OLGA KORBUT

by
Wayne Coffey

BLACKBIRCH PRESS, INC.
Woodbridge, Connecticut

Published by Blackbirch Press, Inc.
One Bradley Road
Woodbridge, CT 06525

©1992 Blackbirch Press, Inc.
First Edition

Manufactured in the United States of America

10 9 8 7 6 5 4 3 2 1

Editor: Bruce Glassman
Photo Research: Grace How
Illustration: Ed Vebell

Library of Congress Cataloging-in-Publication Data
Coffey, Wayne R.
    Olga Korbut / Wayne Coffey. — 1st ed.
    (Olympic Gold)
    Includes bibliographical references and index.
    Summary: A biography of the Soviet gymnast who
won three gold medals in the 1972 Olympics and re-
turned to win another in 1976.
    ISBN 1-56711-002-9
    1.Olga Korbut,1955-   —Juvenile Literature.
2. Gymnasts—Byelarus—Biography—Juvenile litera-
ture. [1. Korbut, Olga, 1955-   . 2. Gymnasts.] I. Title.
II.Series.
GV460.2.K67C64 1992
796.44 '092—dc20
[B]   92-16252
                                                CIP
                                                 AC

Contents

1

Tiny Dynamo

"For me, gymnastics is an expression of my innermost emotions."

ate in the summer of 1972, a buzz of excitement surged through the German city of Munich. Before long, it had spread to the entire world. The enthusiasm was even shared by people who normally weren't avid sports fans. People everywhere couldn't stop talking about the perky, pint-sized girl wonder from the Soviet Union.

Her name was Olga Korbut. She was a gymnast from the town of Grodno, in the far western part of the USSR, just miles from the border of Poland. Before the 1972 Olympic Games were over, millions knew her simply as Olga. As in, "Did you see

Opposite:
Olga's performance in the 1972 Olympics won her three gold medals and the admiration of fans all over the world.

5

what Olga did last night?" "Can you believe this little Olga?"

At four feet, 11 inches and 85 pounds, Olga Korbut was not much bigger than one of the arms of the Soviet weightlifters. She was 17 years old and looked about half that. She was the tiniest Olympian of them all. But that didn't stop her from making a splash worthy of Moby Dick.

Olga Korbut won a total of three gold medals and one silver in those Olympic games. Four years earlier, in Mexico City, Vera Caslavska of Czechoslovakia captured four golds and a silver. In Munich, an East German named Karin Janz won as many individual gold medals as Olga. And Lyudmila Tourischeva, Olga's Soviet teammate, earned the most highly prized title by winning the all-around gymnastic competition.

The Girl in Pigtails

And yet, as the events unfolded, there was no question who the overwhelming favorite was. Olga Korbut's charms were as numerous as her dazzling gymnastics routines. She wore her blonde hair in two little pigtails. She had a broad, bright smile. When she competed, the pigtails bounced behind her. She looked as if she were the happiest girl in the world. And maybe she

was. One motto Olga al-
ways has tried to live by
came from her mother, "Be
careful, be first, be joyful."

At four feet, 11 inches and 85 pounds, Olga Korbut was not much bigger than one of the arms of the Soviet weightlifters.

American television viewers were accustomed to a different sort of Soviet athlete. Many Soviet competitors, it seemed, preferred not to show much emotion. Instead, they would often display a serious, almost mechanical manner. And then, out of nowhere, up pops bouncy little Olga, a bundle of bubbly energy.

A Fearless Competitor

Almost nobody in the United States knew anything about her before the 1972 Games. Olga turned heads quickly. She danced and pranced. She soared and tumbled. She bent her body and bounced about as if she were made of rubber. And the smile seemed to beam all the while. Before the Olympics were over, she had vaulted herself into the hearts of millions.

Another quality of Olga's that made her appealing was that she seemed to have no fear. She would try almost any move. On the four-inch-wide balance beam, she would jump into the air and do a back flip. On the uneven parallel bars, she would execute a "back somersault to a catch"—launching herself high into the air, flipping over

7

backwards, then grabbing the bar on her way down.

Even gymnastics officials and judges were astounded by Olga's daring routines. In fact, some judges were so concerned about the risk involved that they considered banning some stunts in competition.

This was the most important moment in her life. It had turned out all wrong. So Olga cried, and around the world, millions of television viewers shared her hurt.

It was moments after Olga tried one of her back somersaults on the uneven bars that she captured even more hearts. Bumping her foot against the bar, Olga lost her balance and tumbled to the floor. She climbed back up and finished her routine, but later she couldn't hide her disappointment. Tears were streaming down Olga Korbut's cheeks. She had wanted so badly to perform her best. This was the most important moment in her life. It had turned out all wrong. So Olga cried, and around the world, millions of television viewers shared her hurt. Even in making a mistake, Olga Korbut was charming.

"The main thing in gymnastics is to express what one feels," Olga once said. "For me gymnastics is an expression of my innermost emotions." All her emotion was exactly what people responded to.

Olga Korbut came along at a time when relations between the United States and the

Soviet Union were chilly, to say the least. The war in Vietnam was just ending. The two superpowers were very wary of each other. There was deep mistrust, and almost no cooperation.

It was unheard of for a Soviet athlete to become a star in the United States. But that's exactly what Olga Korbut did.

Not long after the Olympics, Olga made a trip to the United States. She received an invitation to visit President Richard Nixon in the White House in Washington, D.C. President Nixon had spent more than 20 years alerting Americans to the dangers posed by communism and the Soviet Union. He had built his political career on the idea that the Soviet Union was an evil empire.

But Olga Korbut went beyond politics. The president had been impressed by her performance in Munich, too. When Olga arrived and they exchanged greetings, the president did a double take. He knew that she was a very petite young woman. But perhaps he didn't quite realize how little 85 pounds really could be.

"My, you're small," President Nixon said to Olga Korbut.

The remarks were translated into Russian. Olga Korbut looked up at the leader of the free world.

"My, you're big," she said with a twinkle.

9

2

Determination and Drive

She wanted to show that just because a person is small doesn't mean she isn't strong or talented.

The town of Grodno is located on the Niemen River, in what is today the republic of Belarus (in the Commonwealth of Independent States). The people there have long been known for their courage and strong-willed characters. They are also known for being extremely self-disciplined and hard-working.

Early in World War II (1939–1945), the Nazi forces of Adolf Hitler invaded the Soviet Union. The first area the powerful German army sought to conquer was Byelorussia (as Belarus was called until recently). The Soviet army was no match for Hitler's troops, but that didn't stop the determined people of the region from fighting bravely to protect their homeland. They refused to give up, no matter how hopeless it seemed. An estimated one million Byelorussians died in the battles with the Germans. Many thousands more were wounded. One of those wounded was a man named Valentin Korbut, Olga's father.

The terrible war had been over for nearly 10 years before Olga was born. But in her own competitive battles, she, too, would go on to show great character and a constant willingness to work.

Childhood in Grodno

Olga Korbut was born on May 16, 1955. She was the youngest of the four daughters of Valentin and his wife, Valentina. After the war, Valentin went to college and became an engineer. Valentina pursued a career in nursing before later becoming a cook.

From the time she was young, Olga's favorite things to do were playing with dolls and going for walks in the vast, thick forest not far from Grodno. There was something she found comforting about the towering trees and the rich smell of the leaves and the earth. It was so peaceful. But before long, Olga had developed another interest as well: sports.

Olga was always, by far, the smallest youngster in her classes. Some of the other kids would make fun of her. They called her names and joked about whether she would ever grow. It was painful for Olga to be different from the rest of the crowd. Sometimes it made her feel like an outcast. It was no fun being picked on.

Many youngsters become very timid when they're teased. But Olga was just the opposite. Her small size only made her more determined. She wanted to show people that just because a person is small doesn't mean she isn't strong or talented.

A Love for Gymnastics

Olga channeled her determination into athletics. She discovered that she loved to run and play. And she was terrific at it, too. On her scrawny little legs, she could run faster than even the biggest girls, and faster than a bunch of the boys, as well. She participated in many sports in school, but her favorite was gymnastics. Olga showed remarkable agility and coordination. It seemed as if she could balance her body on the head of a pencil. She was able to do flips and jumps that her bigger classmates could not do. It didn't take long for her instructors to spot that this little girl was blessed with extraordinary gifts.

When Olga was 10, she was enrolled in a special school for young gymnasts. The leaders of the Soviet government established such schools for a variety of sports. The entrance requirements were very rigid. Only a small percentage of Soviet kids were chosen. The schools were sprinkled throughout the vast nation, which is more than 8 million square miles. Many youngsters traveled hundreds of miles to attend the sports schools. Olga was lucky. There was a gymnastic school right in Grodno.

As a youngster in school, Olga developed a love of sports. She soon found out that she could run faster than most of her schoolmates, including many boys.

Olga's school didn't just offer her intensive instruction in gymnastics. It also put great demands on her schoolwork. But the Soviets believed that students who showed discipline in the classroom would be the ones who performed best in gymnastics.

Rapid Progress and Hard Work

Young Olga thrived in her new school. She studied for hours each day, and she made rapid progress as a gymnast. It helped that she was getting top-flight coaching. Her instructor, Yelena Volchetskaya, was an Olympic star herself. In the 1964 Games in Tokyo, Yelena was part of the Soviet gold-medal winning team. Another coach of Olga's was Tamara Alexeyeva, who was an expert in the horse vault.

Knysh had doubts about Olga, at first. Like so many others, he questioned whether such a small body would have the necessary strength and stamina.

The man in charge of the Grodno school was Renald Knysh, who was one of the best gymnastic instructors in the world. Knysh was constantly on the lookout for new talent. He even kept a record of all the young married couples in Grodno who he felt might give birth to promising gymnasts of the future.

Knysh had doubts about Olga, at first. Like so many others, he questioned whether such a small body would have the necessary strength and stamina. Olga put the questions to rest in no time. Soon, Renald took over Olga's coaching himself.

Renald Knysh is a small, quiet man with deep-set eyes and dark hair. He is totally devoted to his sport. He pushed Olga very hard and demanded total commitment from her. Some coaches scream and criticize their young athletes because they want their students to be terrified of making a mistake. Knysh didn't believe that a temper tantrum would do any good. At the same time, nobody else was stricter or had higher standards.

Renald Knysh's personality was very different from Olga's. Maybe that was why they worked so well together. Olga was much more emotional than her counselor and coach. There were times when he would be watching her from the corner of the gym, arms crossed tightly at his chest, and Olga would be crying or shouting. Sometimes Olga would get into heated disagreements with Renald. She would argue with him about a certain technique, or a new routine he wanted her to perform. Olga had an iron will and could be as stubborn as an ox. When she would get frustrated with long hours of practice, she would insist on doing things the way she wanted. After all, she reasoned, it was she who was performing, not her coach.

15

Olga's fiery nature was a quality her coach greatly admired. It told him how much Olga wanted to succeed. Long before Olga won any Olympic medals, Renald had no doubt that she had the determination and drive of a champion.

Olga's coach, Renald Knysh, was strict and demanding. He always encouraged Olga to try daring new moves that would impress the judges in competition.

It certainly wasn't easy being a pupil of Renald Knysh. He did not believe in doing things the safe, easy way. He was very

creative in his thinking, always probing to refine his students' techniques. He looked for daring new moves that would earn points from judges. Renald didn't believe in simply repeating routines the way they had always been done. And in this sense, he had the perfect pupil in Olga Korbut.

She loved trying new things, too. She found fresh challenges very exciting. If somebody doubted whether she could do something, she would knock herself out to prove him wrong.

She loved trying new things, too. She found fresh challenges very exciting. If somebody doubted whether she could do something, she would knock herself out to prove him wrong. In fact, if Renald had any problem with Olga, it was that she was too eager to experiment with new maneuvers. She had profound self-confidence. Olga didn't want to hear it if Renald said that it was too soon to attempt a certain move. She just wanted to go for it.

The Famous Flip

One of the moves Olga loved the most was the back flip on the balance beam. Renald knew how dangerous the stunt was. But he also knew that Olga's tremendous balance and flexibility—and her determined spirit—made her the ideal candidate to execute it.

The balance beam is a horizontal wooden bar that is only four inches wide. To stand on it, jump in the air, do a back somersault,

and then land squarely on the bar requires expert skill. The move would become one of Olga's trademarks. It established her as one of the leading gymnasts in the world, and also as one of the most courageous. The flip on the beam did not come easily. Day after day, week after week, Olga worked to perfect it. She would practice for hours each day on a variety of moves, but Olga and Renald made sure there was always time to work on her unusual flip.

She was still a very young girl, but Olga Korbut had already learned an important piece of wisdom: If you want to succeed, whether in gymnastics, school, or Chinese Checkers, there's no substitute for hard work.

At times the flip was very trying. She would fall or stumble on her landing. Sometimes she would jump a little awkwardly. This was a trick with no room for error. Olga would get upset occasionally, because of how difficult the back flip was to master. There were times when she was frustrated enough that she felt like telling Renald, "Let's forget the stupid flip. I'm just not getting it." But her perseverance never faltered. Olga would simply climb back up on the beam and keep working at it. She was still a very young girl, but Olga Korbut had already learned an important piece of wisdom: If you want to succeed, whether in gymnastics, school, or Chinese Checkers, there's no substitute for hard work.

Renald studied her closely, breaking the move down to its most simple elements. Gradually, Olga's missteps and mistakes became fewer and fewer. Renald was not the sort of man who would jump for joy when he was happy. But as he watched Olga progress, it was clear he was very pleased. Her hardworking approach was definitely paying off. All he needed to do now was follow her progress.

Ready to Challenge the World

By the time Olga was 15, she had polished her balance-beam back flip and dozens of other moves on the gymnastic equipment. Renald's instincts as a teacher told him his prize pupil was ready for even greater challenges. He wanted to enter her in bigger, tougher meets, in which she would compete against some of the finest gymnasts in the world. He decided that Olga was ready to try the back flip in open competition. The new experience could only help her to improve her techniques.

Little Olga Korbut was thrilled when her coach told her of his plans. In his own reserved way, Renald Knysh was raring to go, too. They had had many rehearsals over the years. The preparation was completed, and the pieces were all in place. Now it was time for the show to begin.

3

A Turning Point

"We only want to protect you."

The Soviet Union held a championship gymnastics meet every year. This was the competition Renald Knysh wanted Olga to enter. The only problem was that the USSR Championship meet was limited to athletes 16 years or older. Olga was still just 15.

Knysh had to see if he could get officials to bend the rule to allow Olga to compete. He talked it over with Larissa Latynina, the coach of the USSR women's national team. They agreed that Olga had the talent to participate in the meet. Larissa had seen some of Olga's practices and came away very impressed. She had rarely seen such a bold and skillful young gymnast. To the women's coach, Olga's age was unimportant. Olga Korbut belonged in the meet. After several discussions, meet officials agreed and suspended the age limit just for Olga.

A Remarkable Premiere

If Olga Korbut was nervous going into the biggest competition of her life, you'd never have known it. Olga finished in fifth place overall, an astounding feat in view of the tough level of competition. She had even surpassed several women who had won medals in the Mexico City Olympic Games the year before.

The youngest and smallest gymnast of all was the one everyone was talking about. Her back flip on the balance beam had left people with their eyes wide and jaws open. Nobody had ever seen such a thing. On the uneven bars, she had displayed similar courage and skill, flipping and whirling around as if there were no such thing as gravity. Her performance had been so breathtaking that some people felt the judges had slighted her. One theory was that Olga's moves were too new and creative to win the judges' approval. The judges knew that Renald Knysh was always searching for innovations, but this time

some judges felt he had gone too far. They believed Olga's routine was more fitting for a circus than a gymnastics meet.

Renald didn't let these criticisms bother him. Olga wasn't upset, either. Why should she have been? Her gymnastics career could hardly have been going better. The following year, 1970, she captured a gold medal in the vault at the Soviet national meet. She placed fourth overall. When it was time to select the team members for the world championship meet later that year in Yugoslavia, Olga Korbut was impossible to ignore. She had proven herself to be one of the outstanding gymnasts in the country.

Disappointment in Yugoslavia

The top Soviet coaches and officials had just one concern. Because Olga was so young, they questioned whether she had the maturity and poise to compete in such a distinguished event. They did not want to rush her. The most important thing, they felt, was to let her continue to progress at her own pace.

After weighing all the factors, the officials decided that Olga would not represent the Soviet Union at the world championships. They explained their reasoning to her in detail. They assured her it had nothing to do with her gymnastic skills. After all, they

told Olga over and over again, they knew what a wonderful gymnast she was.

"We only want to protect you," they said.

Olga traveled to Yugoslavia, anyway, because her coaches felt it would be good for her to be exposed to the atmosphere of such a big meet. While she was there, she performed in some exhibitions for a panel of judges. The judges were thoroughly impressed with young Olga Korbut. And they told her so.

Olga was hearing so many flattering things that she started to get a swelled head. She became boastful. She resented that she

In 1970, Olga traveled to Yugoslavia with the Soviet team, but only as an observer. The top coaches and officials from the USSR had decided that Olga would not be included in the world championship competition.

wasn't allowed to compete. Olga bragged about her accomplishments, even telling some of her teammates that the only reason they were participating was because she had been left out.

Attitude Problems

She had never had any problems making friends or getting along with her teammates before. But suddenly, Olga had big problems. Her teammates didn't care for her big-shot attitude. They didn't appreciate that she seemed to think she was the queen of the gymnastics world.

Olga's teammates began to shun her. Nobody wanted to be friends with a brat, which is what Olga was behaving like.

Renald Knysh and Olga's family firmly told Olga she had no right to act in such a manner. They made it clear to her that criticizing her teammates was not nice, or smart. Still, this was a lesson Olga had to learn for herself.

Olga's teammates began to shun her. Nobody wanted to be friends with a brat, which is what Olga was behaving like. It was a very difficult time for her. Things got even harder when she became ill and had to take some time off from training.

Olga was miserable about not being able to practice. She was also unhappy about not being accepted by her teammates. It was robbing her of the joys of

companionship and team-
work. It was no fun not having
people to talk to or even to
kid around with. Olga came

She learned the value of friendships. And she learned that having team spirit was what sports were all about.

to realize how important the other girls'
support was to her. She learned the value
of friendships. And she learned that having
team spirit was what sports were all about.

It was a big turning point in Olga's
growth as a person. She didn't want to go
her own way anymore. She just wanted to
be one of the girls.

Her teammates were very understanding.
When they saw that Olga had changed,
they accepted her back. The wounds healed
quickly. Olga could go back to concentrat-
ing on her gymnastics—for the time being.
She didn't know it then, but another
personal turning point was soon to follow.
It would happen in the city of Munich.

4

Rise and Fall

"I need something I can really put all my heart and emotions into."

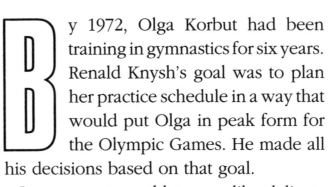

y 1972, Olga Korbut had been training in gymnastics for six years. Renald Knysh's goal was to plan her practice schedule in a way that would put Olga in peak form for the Olympic Games. He made all his decisions based on that goal.

In a sense, top athletes are like delicate musical instruments. They need to be very finely tuned to perform their best. All parts must be in top condition. An athlete can't simply expect to step into a competition without any preparation and do well. You wouldn't expect much from a guitar that has been sitting in the back of a closet for the last two years.

At the same time, most athletes have to be careful *In a sense, top athletes are like delicate musical instruments.* not to overdo their preparation. Too much practice can result in injuries. It can also leave the athlete mentally and physically drained.

The more he observed Olga, the more Renald was convinced she was exactly where she needed to be. Olga's workouts were steadily improving. Her concentration—a critical part of gymnastics—was excellent.

A Big Victory in Riga

In July 1972, Olga competed in a major international tournament called the USSR Union Cup. It was held in the city of Riga, in the region of the USSR known as Latvia. (Latvia is now an independent country, having broken away from the other Soviet republics during the political changes that occurred late in the summer of 1991.) Olga achieved a big upset, winning the all-around title. To do it, she outperformed two more experienced and more famous teammates: Lyudmila Tourischeva and Tamara Lazakovitch.

With this stunning victory, Olga assured herself a spot in the Olympics. She continued to work hard to perfect her routines in all four individual exercises: the balance

beam, uneven parallel bars, the horse vault, and floor exercise.

Along with her Soviet teammates, Olga was prepared for the Olympics by a group of advisers. There were not only coaches in this group. There also were choreographers, who helped refine the athletes' movements to make them more graceful. There was even a sports psychologist, who helped the athletes maintain a positive frame of mind.

A Change of Heart

Everything was going well—until five days before the team was due to depart for the Olympics. Olga dropped a bombshell on Renald Knysh. She told him she didn't like the musical selection for her floor exercise program. The piece was called "Flight of the Bumble Bee." It had been selected especially for Olga by coach Larissa Latynina, who thought it was ideal for her. So did everybody else. Except Olga.

Olga had been working on the routine for months. Hours of painstaking effort had been invested in the preparation. But Olga didn't care about that right now. She wanted to scrap the music and come up with a new selection.

Renald tried to talk her out of it. Olga would not budge. With the same iron will that helped make her a first-rate gymnast, she was standing by her instincts. She felt the piece didn't fit her personality.

"I need something I can really put all my heart and emotions into," Olga said.

Knysh was thoroughly frustrated over Olga's stubbornness. He was certain that Olga was risking her chance of winning a medal in the Olympics. But he knew better than to get into a battle of wills with her.

Five days before the team was supposed to leave for the 1972 Olympics, Olga decided to change the music for her floor exercise. Although her coach tried to talk her out of it, Olga would not change her mind.

The truth was that Olga was right about one thing; if her heart really wasn't in "Flight of the Bumble Bee," it would show up in her final performance.

After many tense discussions, Renald reluctantly gave Olga new music and a new routine for her floor exercise. She immediately went to work on it in the gym. She practiced for hours and hours and made terrific progress. Still, the amount of time she had was a fraction of what was needed to master it.

Olga didn't let this bother her. She was certain she had made the right move. When the Olympic Games in Munich began, her outlook was very upbeat.

A Stunning Display in Munich

The first Olympic event was the individual all-around, in which gymnasts competed in all four exercises: the balance beam, the parallel bars, the vault, and the floor routine. The competitor with the highest combined score is chosen as the all-around gymnastic champion.

Olga got off to a superb start. Already, the huge crowd loved her smile and spirit, the joyful bounce in her movements.

Olga executed a fine vault. It placed her among the leaders. On the balance beam, she was even better. She highlighted a stunning display with her back somersault. The move had become an Olga Korbut trademark among gymnastics insiders, but the Munich crowd had never seen it before. The awestruck fans let out a loud gasp when she leaped off the bar and whirled backwards in the air, before landing smoothly back onto the four-inch-wide beam.

When Olga bounded off to conclude her exercise, she planted herself squarely on the ground. She raised her arms over her head and fluttered her hands as if they were leaves on a tree. The crowd went wild. Olga's ears were filled with louder cheers than she had ever heard before.

Her scores placed her in an excellent position for a medal in the all-around. She was up there with Lyudmila and Tamara.

Olga's next challenge was the uneven bars, one of her strongest events. Here, too, Olga had developed a daring stunt. It was the back somersault to a catch, an extremely difficult move made as she swung from the higher bar to the lower one. With

The awestruck fans let out a loud gasp when she leaped off the bar and whirled backward in the air, before landing smoothly back onto the four-inch-wide beam.

her confidence soaring after the balance beam, Olga was excited about wowing the crowd some more.

Olga gripped the bar and started her routine. She stumbled slightly as she swung

into her first move. It was a small mistake, but still a mistake. Olga was very angry at herself for making it. The slip-up seemed to throw off her concentration. She mishandled the bar as she executed another move, and this made her even more upset. She was shaken. Then, as she was about to perform the somersault, she lost her balance. She desperately grabbed at the bar. She couldn't get it. She fell off, tumbling to the ground.

Olga was devastated. She completed her routine and then ran to the bench and began to weep. The judges had given her a score of 7.50—the perfect score is 10. It was fair, considering her errors. Her dream of an all-around medal was over. There was no way she could finish in the top three with such a low score in one event.

Suddenly, everything had gone all wrong. Her confidence had been shattered.

More events were yet to come. There was plenty of time left for Olga to settle down and try to put this awful memory behind her. But was this 17-year-old girl mature enough to do it? Could she rise above her disappointment, regain her concentration, and give her best effort? As little Olga sat slumped on the bench, tears tracing down her cheeks, it seemed extremely doubtful.

(Continued on page 49)

1972

MUNICH, GERMANY

WITH FAMILY AND FRIENDS

In her private life, Olga has always been regarded by those who know her as "down to earth" and charming. *Above:* Olga serves tea to her father, mother, and sister during breakfast at their home in Grodno, 1973. *Left:* Olga attends a history class in Moscow a few months after her triumphs in the 1972 Olympic Games. *Right:* Classmates gather around to speak with one of the Soviet Union's favorite gymnasts.

FEARLESS AND FANTASTIC

When Olga entered the world gymnastic scene, she became an instant sensation. One thing that made her so appealing was her apparent fearlessness in her routines. *Above:* On the balance beam, Olga combined daring jumps with perfect form. *Right:* Because she was small and light, Olga was able to achieve breathtaking heights on her leaps. *Opposite:* Olga's "back somersault to a catch" on the uneven parallel bars was one of her most astounding maneuvers.

THE EYES OF THE WORLD

One of the most difficult parts of any gymnastic routine is the dismount, or ending. Landing firmly on two feet while holding form was another of Olga's natural abilities. *Opposite inset:* Olga sits among the thousands of letters from fans that poured in after her victories in 1972. *Opposite:* Soviet weightlifter Vassily Alexeyev dwarfs Olga at an Olympic press conference.

LIFE AS A SOVIET GYMNAST

Hard work, determination, and a great competitive drive are important qualities for an Olympic champion. *Above:* Olga discusses her routine with coach Renald Knysh. *Below:* Olympic star, Nelli Kim asks advice from her coach and choreographer. *Opposite:* Lyudmila Tourischeva was one of the world's leading gymnasts, however, she never achieved Olga's popularity.

A WIFE AND A MOTHER

Two years after her final competition in the 1976 Olympics, Olga married Soviet musician Leonid Bortkevich. They were wed in a small ceremony in Minsk, the capital of Byelorussia. *Inset:* Olga and her husband pose with Nelli Kim and their newly born son, Richard, in 1979.

LIFE TODAY

Olga's Olympic glory days have faded into the past, but she remains active and involved in the world of athletics. Even though she is no longer competing, Olga still stays in shape by stretching and exercising regularly.

45

OLD WORK, NEW DIRECTIONS

In recent years, Olga has begun to teach gymnastics to a new generation of young rising stars. The great wealth of knowledge that Olga gained during her days as a top athlete is one of the most valuable things she can pass on to others.

OLGA IN THE USA

In 1989, Olga traveled to New York with her family to join other world-class athletes in the Gymnastics '89 Tour of Champions. Olga arrived at John F. Kennedy airport with her husband, Leonid, and her son, Richard.

(Continued from page 32)

5

Triumph

"I won't make any more blunders. I simply won't."

I f Olga Korbut was going to rebound from her disaster, she was going to have to do it very quickly. The next phase of competition, the individual events, were being held the next day. Olga didn't even have a full 24 hours before having to return to the scene of her tears.

She spent the night in the Olympic village. Her teammates were extremely kind and supportive of her. They listened to her concerns and they told her that even the greatest gymnasts make mistakes. They did their best to convince Olga not to be too critical of herself. One of the most understanding friends of all was Lyudmila

Tourischeva, who went on to win the gold medal after Olga's slip-up. Lyudmila was regarded as the finest female gymnast in the world. She let Olga know that she had complete faith that Olga could come out the next day and put the disappointment behind her.

Mustering Courage

Later that night, Olga did an interview for television. "I won't make any more blunders," she said, "I simply won't." Olga sounded very confident as she uttered the words. But you knew that, deep down, the self-doubts had to remain.

When Olga arrived with her teammates at the hall the next day, she could feel the eyes of the crowd on her. Olga Korbut had become the talk of the gymnastic competition. She was the overwhelming crowd favorite. Olga was so much the center of attention that television broadcaster Jim McKay jokingly called the telecast "The Olga Korbut Show."

On that day, August 31, 1972, the Olga Korbut Show was in all its glory. On the balance beam, she danced and bounced with almost effortless grace. She showed remarkable poise and precision. And then, near the close of her routine,

Olga was so much the center of attention that television broadcaster Jim McKay jokingly called the telecast "The Olga Korbut Show."

she coiled her tiny body and jumped up, spinning backwards into her somersault. She came down right on the beam. The crowd exploded in applause. The arena was almost shaking from the noise.

One of Olga's most astounding moves on the balance beam was her backwards somersault.

When the judges awarded her the top score of the day, the cheering became even louder. Tamara Lazakovitch, her teammate, and several others also performed well. But nobody could match Olga. Nobody else had a back somersault in her routine. Olga Korbut had won a gold medal. It was the greatest thrill she had experienced in all her years of competing.

And she wasn't done yet. She turned her energies toward the uneven bars—the site

of her tears the day before. Olga needed nearly a perfect 10.0 score to beat Karin Janz of East Germany.

She whipped under and over and through the bars. It was as if the fall had never happened. With each successful stunt, Olga's confidence soared. As she flew off the bars in a grand finale, she saluted the crowd and knew she had done her best. Again, the hall erupted in cheers.

The Crowd Votes for Olga

The judges tallied Olga's scores and posted the mark—a 9.80. It was a very fine score. The only problem was that Olga needed 9.90 or better to surpass Karin Janz.

Gymnastics crowds are usually very polite, but the Munich throng wasn't thinking about good manners at this point. These people were in love with Olga Korbut and they wanted her to win.

At 17, with the whole world watching, Olga Korbut had handled the pressure of the Olympics as if she had been doing it her whole life.

People hooted and hollered at the judges. They stomped their feet on the wooden floorboards. At times it seemed as if a riot might break out, people were so upset about Olga's score. Nobody listened when officials pleaded for quiet. They explained that this behavior was very unfair to the other competitors, which was absolutely right. Still, the crowd was stomping.

The din did not die down until the next competitor was finished with her routine. The judges would not consider changing Olga's score. Olga finished with 19.45 total points, just short of Karin Janz's 19.675.

But even if the boisterous crowd wasn't happy, Olga had to feel great satisfaction. She had won the silver medal. She had not only gotten back on the bars that had left her so distraught a day earlier, but she had also responded with one of her finest efforts ever. At 17, with the whole world watching, Olga Korbut had handled the pressure of the Olympics as if she had been doing it her whole life.

The Final Event

The only event that remained was the floor exercise. It was usually Olga's strongest event, because it was the one place where all her sparkle and girlish charm could come out.

Olga was performing to the new musical selection after her last-minute switch. It didn't seem to bother her at all. Olga displayed a stunning blend of grace and agility. She was full of spirit and joy. She bounced and flipped, tumbled and twirled— all in perfect time with the music.

Her performance was happy. It was light. It seemed to put glee in the heart of every

Olga gave a stunning performance with her floor exercise in the 1972 Games. The judges rewarded her with a score of 9.90.

last person in the hall. If she weren't 17, she probably could've been elected mayor of Munich that night.

The massive crowd let out a deafening roar when she finished. They let out another one when the judges posted her score: 9.90! Nobody was going to duplicate that. Olga Korbut had captured her second gold medal of the 1972 Olympic Games. And she won a third gold, as a member of the victorious Soviet team. When you count the silver she took on the uneven bars, her total was four medals.

The World's Little Girl

To millions of viewers and fans around the world, it wasn't the medals that made Olga Korbut so enchanting. For three days, it was as if she were the whole world's little girl. People loved her sunny spirit and daring maneuvers. They loved the way she smiled, and they wanted to hug her when she cried. Perhaps most of all, though, people admired her for her courage. After her humiliating fall, it would have been very easy to quit. Some observers said that Olga might not even show up the next day.

Back when Renald Knysh first started working with Olga, he saw a champion's determination in the little girl from Grodno. He knew that she had something special inside her. After seven years of work, Olga Korbut proved exactly how right Renald had been all along. And she proved it on the biggest stage in the world: the Olympic Games.

People admired her for her courage. After her humiliating fall, it would have been very easy to quit.

6

Moving On

"Be careful, be first, be joyful."

t didn't take long for the honors to begin pouring in for Olga Korbut. Unknown before the Olympics, she had become the most talked-about athlete in the world. She had a stack of newspaper clippings as thick as a phone book. Early in 1973, the Associated Press conducted an international poll. The wire news service voted Olga Korbut its female Athlete of the Year. It marked the first time in more than 40 years that an athlete from a Communist country had received the noteworthy honor.

Six months after the Games, the Soviet gymnastics team made a whirlwind tour of the United States. The team visited 8 cities in 17 days. There were 15 members in the troop, but there was no doubt who the leading attraction was.

An American Sensation

Olga was mobbed by fans everywhere she went. She learned that Olga Korbut fan clubs were springing up all over the United States. In New York, 19,694 people jammed into Madison Square Garden to catch a glimpse of Olga and her teammates. It was the largest crowd ever to watch a gymnastics event in the western hemisphere.

"America is different than I expected," she said. "I like it."

New York Mayor John Lindsay gave her the key to the city. In Chicago, Mayor Richard Daley declared it "Olga Korbut Day" when the team arrived. Flashbulbs popped all around her. Reporters asked her question after question. One of the questions was what she thought of the United States.

"America is different than I expected," she said. "I like it." She may have liked the food most of all. She devoured peanuts and pretzels, and she discovered American ice cream was tasty, too. The Soviet gymnasts were supposed to be on a strict diet, but this did not appear to stop her. Olga's favorite food of all was ketchup. She couldn't get

enough of it. She put it on almost every-thing. One time, she poured it on top of a stack of pancakes.

Later Victories

Olga captured many more medals over the next few years after Munich. She com-peted in the 1976 Olympics in Montreal, where she again was part of the gold-medal winning Soviet team.

But four years is a long time in the life of a competitive athlete. Olga Korbut was not quite the same electrifying performer she had been in Munich. Her only individual medal in Montreal was a silver on the balance beam.

A new Soviet youngster, Nelli Kim, was making a big sensation. And Lyudmila Tourischeva remained one of the best in the world. The biggest star in Montreal, though, was a new pint-sized wonder. She, too, was four feet, 11 inches. Her name was

Olga Korbut was not quite the same electrifying performer she had been in Munich.

Nadia Comaneci. She was from Romania, and she was just 14 years old. Nadia not only won the gold medal in the all-around, she did it by receiving the first 10.0 scores for the event in Olympic history.

People made the obvious comparisons between Nadia and Olga. Both girls were the size of dolls, and both were from

Communist countries. Many fans were calling Nadia "the new Olga Korbut."

Nadia Comaneci put on one of the greatest performances in Olympic history in the Montreal Games. Her scores easily surpassed those of Olga from 1972. They left no doubt that Nadia was the best gymnast in the world.

It wasn't easy for Olga to be in somebody else's shadow. It stung her pride that she wasn't the main attraction any longer. Olga did her best to accept that this was the way it was in sports. New, determined challengers are always coming along.

Olga earned many more medals for gymnastics after the 1972 Munich Games. In addition to winning a few international competitions, Olga was part of the gold-medal Soviet team in the 1976 Olympics.

Olga did not appear in any other Olympics after that. She retired from the sport and dreamed of becoming an actress, though that dream never materialized. Olga got married and gave birth to a son. She also moved to the city of Minsk, the capital of Byelorussia. Then, nearly 10 years after her last Olympics, Olga wound up living through a frightening ordeal.

Terror in Chernobyl

In April 1986, one of the worst nuclear accidents in history occurred in the Soviet city of Chernobyl. Minsk was close enough to the damaged plant that its residents were affected by the leaking radiation. Olga has told reporters that she suffers from a thyroid problem and exhaustion as a result of the accident. She and her family came to the United States for a thorough examination in 1991, and no further effects were discovered. Whether there are complications in the future remains to be seen.

Olga's visit to America was just more evidence of what a legend she became in Munich. Almost 20 years later, her name was still big news—even if the news, in this instance, was far from happy.

There's no disputing that the feats of Nadia Comaneci in 1976 were astounding.

But there's also no question that in Munich, Germany, Olga Korbut secured her own spot in Olympic history. She had stirred the passions of the crowd as they had never been stirred before. Single-handedly, Olga made gymnastics a widely popular spectator sport. In three days' time, she had created her own little revolution.

A Special Place in History

An estimated half billion people watched her on television in 1972. Many of them still have vivid memories of those bouncing pigtails and the glowing smile that beamed out from her tiny body. They remember the daring stunts, the tears, and the way she came back to triumph a day later. They remember a warm and cuddly little girl who bounced right into their hearts. This tiny dynamo made people realize that bigger may not be better when it comes to sports champions.

Single-handedly, Olga made gymnastics a widely popular spectator sport. In three days' time, she had created her own little revolution.

Olga Korbut loved playing with dolls in her childhood. Now, here she was, the world's doll. Olga always tried to remember her mother's advice: "Be careful, be first, be joyful."

In Munich in 1972, Olga was three-for-three. That's a perfect score any way you count it.

61

Glossary

agility Ability to move quickly and gracefully

balance beam A four-inch-wide wooden bar used for gymnastic routines.

blunders Mistakes.

boisterous Noisy and excited.

Commonwealth of Independent States A loose association of 11 of the Soviet Union's former republics that was founded in 1991.

dynamo A bundle of energy.

innovations New ideas.

Nazis The German political party that was in power during the 1930s and the 1940s led by Adolf Hitler. One of the ultimate goals of the Nazi party was the extermination of the Jewish people.

perserverance Determinaton and drive.

somersault A rotating flip in the air.

stamina Strength and endurance.

thyroid A gland in the body that produces a hormone that regulates metabolism.

vault An element of most gymnastic competitions where the gymnast runs, leaps in the air, and performs somersaults before a final landing.

For Further Reading

Arnold, Caroline. *The Olympic Summer Games*. New York: Franklin Watts, 1991.

Arnold, Caroline. *The Olympic Winter Games*. New York: Franklin Watts, 1991.

Murdock, Tony, and Stuart, Nik. *Gymnastics*. New York: Franklin Watts, 1989.

Tatlow, Peter. *Gymnastics*. Westwood: Silver Burdett Press, 1989.

Tatlow, Peter. *The Olympics*. New York: Franklin Watts, 1988.

Index

Photo Credits

Front and back covers: Sovoto; front cover (inset):
©Y. Somov/Sovfoto; p. 4: ©N. Naumenkov/Sovfoto;
p. 33: Popperfoto; pp. 34 (top), 35, 39: ©Yu. Morgulis/
Sovfoto; p. 34 (bottom): ©V. Sozinov/Sovfoto; pp. 36
(top and bottom), 37, 41: Sovfoto; p. 39: ©Y. Somov/
Sovfoto; p. 40 (top): ©V. Un Da-Sin/Sovfoto; p. 40
(bottom): ©I. Budnevich/Sovfoto; pp. 42–43: ©Yu.
Ivanov/Sovfoto; p. 42 (inset): ©N. Petropavlovski/
Sovfoto; pp. 44, 45, 46–47: ©Yvonne Hemsey/Gamma-
Liaison; p. 48: AP/Wide World Photos.